AMBER
FORT

DORLING KINDERSLEY
London, New York, Munich,
Melbourne and Delhi

Head of Publishing	Aparna Sharma
Art Director	Shefali Upadhyay
Design Manager	Arunesh Talapatra
Designers	Neerja Rawat,
	Mini Dhawan
Editors	Dipali Singh, Saloni Talwar,
	Suchismita Banerjee
Production Manager	Pankaj Sharma
DTP Designers	Jagtar Singh, Dheeraj Arora
	Harish Aggarwal
Photographers	Gary Ombler

First published in India in 2008
by Dorling Kindersley (India) Pvt. Limited
in association with Penquin Book India (P) Ltd.,
11, Community Centre, Panchsheel Park, New Delhi - 110017
Copyright © 2008 Dorling Kindersley (India) Pvt. Limited

ISBN 978-0-14-306553-1

Printed and bound in
Gopsons Papers Ltd., Noida, India

Discover more at
www.dk.com

Discover more at
www.penguinbooksindia.com

AMBER
FORT

A Mighty Sentinel

Historically, Rajasthan was never unified as a single state. Instead, over the centuries, the region was divided into a number of kingdoms presided over by Rajput warrior families, who fought with each other for supremacy, but also united against such common enemies as the neighbouring sultans of Delhi. This more or less continuous state of warfare also characterized the Rajput relationship with the Mughals in the 16th and 17th centuries, despite marriage alliances between the Rajputs and Mughal emperors. It explains why Rajput forts and palaces were conceived as formidable citadels, elevated on hilltops that overlooked the cities below. Among the most imposing of these forts in Rajasthan is that at Amber, headquarters of the Kachhwaha rulers from the beginning of the 16th century until their move in 1727 to the newly planned city of Jaipur, a short distance away. The Amber Fort is built as a series of courtyards ascending a steep hill that overlooks a strategic pass, through which the highway to Delhi runs. Developed by two Kachhwaha rulers, Man Singh (r.1590–1615) and Mirza Jai Singh (r.1621–1667), into a showpiece of Rajput strength and magnificence. The fort has sumptuous halls, apartments, and pavilions facing onto paved courtyards and formal gardens with pools, water channels, and fountains. The carved marble panels, inlaid mirrorwork, and vivid murals imitate the decoration of Mughal palaces. This is not surprising, since Man Singh and Mirza Jai Singh were commanders in the army of the Mughal emperors, at a time when Mughal influence was strong.

• Jaipur

⚜ **RAJPUT CITADEL**
Amber was the seat of the Rajputs before the capital shifted to Jaipur.

The Rajputs of Amber

Rajputs are believed to have a long geneaology; some of the warrior clans are of the Sun dynasty, others of the Moon. The Kachhwahas are *suryavanshi* (of the Sun dynasty), tracing their descent from Kush, son of Lord Rama. They came into prominence in the tenth century as the rulers of Gwalior in central India, but in 986, Ishwar Das, the king of Gwalior, abdicated to lead a life of renunciation in the Himalayas. His sons moved to the west (present-day Rajasthan), after being forced to flee from Gwalior by their uncle. One of them, Sodh Rai, defeated the Meenas, the tribal chiefs of Dausa (near modern Jaipur) and set up a principality there. In 1037, his son and grandson, Dhola Rai and Kakil Dev, occupied the Meena stronghold at Amber and made it the capital of the Kachhwahas. The clan ruled for centuries, gaining in strength in the 16th century when they formed alliances with the Mughal emperors. Listed below are some of the rulers of Amber:

- 1036–1038 **Kakil Dev**
  Conquers Amber with his father. Builds a fort there.

- 1548–1574 **Bharmal Singh**
  Gains power for Amber by entering into a political alliance with the Mughals.

- 1590–1615 **Man Singh I**
  Begins building the Amber Fort in 1592 on the ruins of Kakil Dev's fort.

- 1622–1668 **Jai Singh I**
  Completes construction of the Amber Fort.

- 1700–1744 **Jai Singh II**
  Moves the capital from Amber to Jainagara (present-day Jaipur) in 1727.

Fort on a Hill

The picturesque Amber Fort stretches across a rocky hill overlooking a gorge, in which the Maota Lake nestles. The town of Amber was founded by the Meena chief, Raja Alan Singh, and was dedicated to Amba, the Mother Goddess, from whom it gets its name. By 967, Amber was a flourishing settlement. In 1037, it was conquered by the Kachhwaha Rajputs, who ruled till 1727. The present citadel was built in 1592, but most of its splendid palaces, pavilions, and gardens were created by Jai Singh I.

Raja Man Singh I

A warrior and wise administrator, Raja Man Singh I was one of the *navratnas* (nine gems) in the court of Mughal emperor Akbar. Commander-in-chief in the Mughal army, he fought in many Mughal campaigns, often emerging as victor. With varied interests, such as art, crafts, literature, and the performing arts, he was a multi-faceted personality. For his kingdom, he was an absentee ruler, carrying out his duties in the army and as governor of the provinces of Kabul, Bihar, and Bengal, but the Kachhwaha principality expanded during his rule.

THE TOWN OF AMBER
This historic town lies on the site (the foothills below the Amber Fort) of the early capital of the Kachhwaha kings.

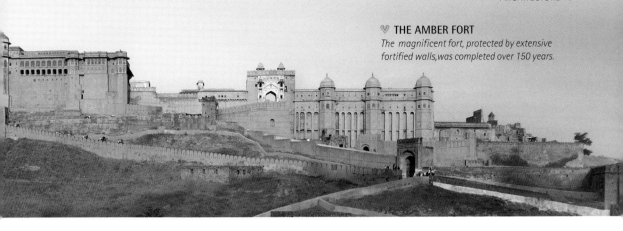

❀ THE AMBER FORT
The magnificent fort, protected by extensive fortified walls, was completed over 150 years.

Raja Jai Singh I and II

The title of honour "Mirza" was conferred on Raja Jai Singh I by Shah Jahan, in recognition of his bravery in battles during the Mughal military campaigns (he served under three Mughal emperors – Jahangir, Shah Jahan, and Aurangzeb). His namesake, Raja Jai Singh II, would later build Jaipur – he was given the title of "Sawai" (one and a quarter times superior to everyone) by Aurangzeb. The two Jai Singhs were the greatest builders among the Kachhwahas, exhibiting a talent for architectural design.

✑ RAJA JAI SINGH II
The Raja shifted the capital to Jaipur in 1727 and built several splendid palaces there.

CHANDRA MAHAL ✑
This grand palace of Raja Jai Singh II in Jaipur is now home to the royal family of Jaipur.

CONNECTING WITH THE MUGHALS

The Kachhwahas recognized the expediency of aligning themselves with the powerful Mughal emperors. The astute diplomatic move of Raja Bharmal, who gave his daughter in marriage to the Mughal emperor Akbar, resulted in the Amber royal family's prominence as did Raja Man Singh and Raja Jai Singh I's feats of valour in the Mughal army. The Rajas also adopted Mughal craft skills, such as *meenakari* (enamel work) in jewellery.

⚜ MEENAKARI
Fine meenakari work introduced by Mughal craftsmen is now part of Rajput tradition.

Forts and Palaces

The Rajputs have always been great patrons of art and architecture. Since they were essentially warriors, forts have always been the focal point of their settlements. Constructed as inner citadels, surrounded by a town and enclosed by a fortified wall, they were usually built on hills for natural protection, and surrounded by wide moats to make them impregnable. Opulent palaces were built within the forts in a sophisticated architectural style – with distinctive indigenous features (see below) that were influenced by Persian and Mughal architecture, particularly in the use of domes and arches. Some of the finest Rajput forts and palaces can be seen in cities such as Jaisalmer, Jodhpur, Udaipur, and Jaipur.

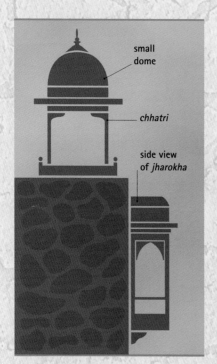

small dome

chhatri

side view of *jharokha*

ARCHITECTURAL FEATURES
The chhatri *(kiosk) and* jharokha *(protruding balcony) are typical elements of the Rajput style.*

The Entrance

Winding up the hillside, the cobbled road leads to the Suraj Pol (Sun Gate), the main entrance gate. It is called so because it faces the direction of the rising sun, the Kachhwaha family emblem. A royal way to reach the Suraj

Pol is to ride up on one of the colourfully caparisoned elephants waiting at the foothill, just as the kings did. This gate opens into the Jaleb Chowk, the courtyard where elephants and horses used to be tethered.

SURAJ POL
Sturdy parapets surmount the arches of this imposing gateway, balanced by graceful chhatris.

Chand Pol

Across the Jaleb Chowk, opposite the Suraj Pol, is the Chand Pol (Moon Gate), which was the main entrance for commoners. The upper storey, from where kettle drums and other musical instruments were played, is the Naubat Khana (Drum House). Next to the gate are the quarters for the elephants and horses. A stone path through Chand Pol leads to the ancient temples and other remains of the old town outside the fort.

jharokha

Singh Pol

A broad flight of steps towards the corner of Jaleb Chowk leads to the double gateway of the Singh Pol (Lion Gate). Built by Raja Ram Singh I, son of Raja Jai Singh I, this gateway has two arches and is decorated with frescoes. Crowned with a *jharokha* in true Rajput style, it is flanked by two *chhatris*. Next to this gateway stands the temple of the family deity of the Kachhwahas, which is called the Shila Devi Temple. The interiors of this temple are decorated with exquisite marble work. The Singh Pol leads to the imperial quarters of the fort.

THE SHILA DEVI LEGEND

The Shila Devi Temple is an impressive shrine featuring silver doors with deities displayed in raised relief work. The temple is named after Shila Devi ("Shila" means stone slab and "Devi" means goddess). According to legend, Raja Man Singh I prayed to the goddess, seeking victory over the rulers of Bengal. She appeared in his dream and asked him to recover her statue submerged in the sea near Jessore (now in Bangladesh) and install it in a temple. The Raja recovered the statue after subjugating his enemies and had this temple constructed.

꘎ **SINGH POL**
A jharokha sits atop the arch of this gate.

꘎ **JALEB CHOWK**
This vast courtyard was the parade ground where the royal armies would assemble; it is lined with barracks.

FRESCO IN NICHE

relief carving

SILVER DOOR

Layout of the Amber Fort complex

The massive ramparts of the Amber Fort follow the contours of the hill on which it stands. The fort is a splendid complex of gateways, courts, stairways, pillared pavilions, and palaces that recall the glory and wealth of Amber's former rulers. The imperial section consists of private palaces for men, apartments for the royal women and their attendants, and landscaped gardens with water channels and stone-trimmed flowerbeds. The gardens surround the Maota Lake.

COMPLEX PLAN

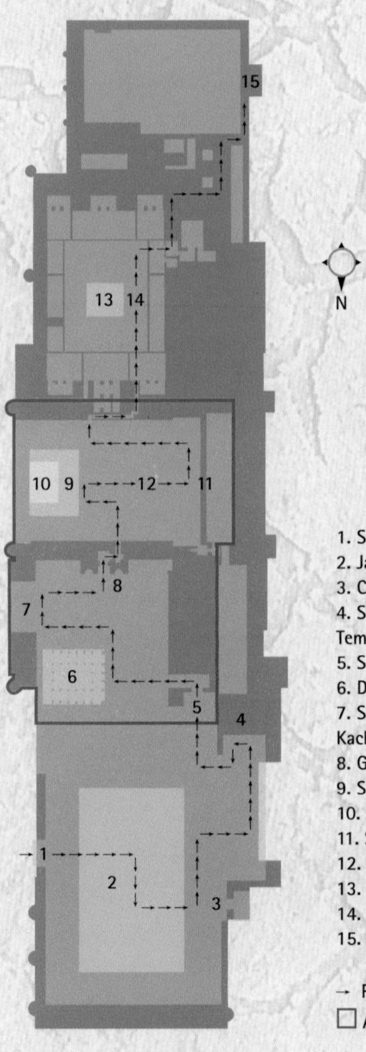

N

1. Suraj Pol
2. Jaleb Chowk
3. Chand Pol
4. Shila Devi Temple
5. Singh Pol
6. Diwan-i-Aam
7. Sattais Kacheri
8. Ganesh Pol
9. Sheesh Mahal
10. Jas Mandir
11. Sukh Niwas
12. Aram Bagh
13. Baradari
14. Zenana
15. Rang Mahal

→ Path through the fort
☐ Area illustrated above

Aram Bagh

Sheesh Mahal

Jas Mandir

Sattais Kacheri

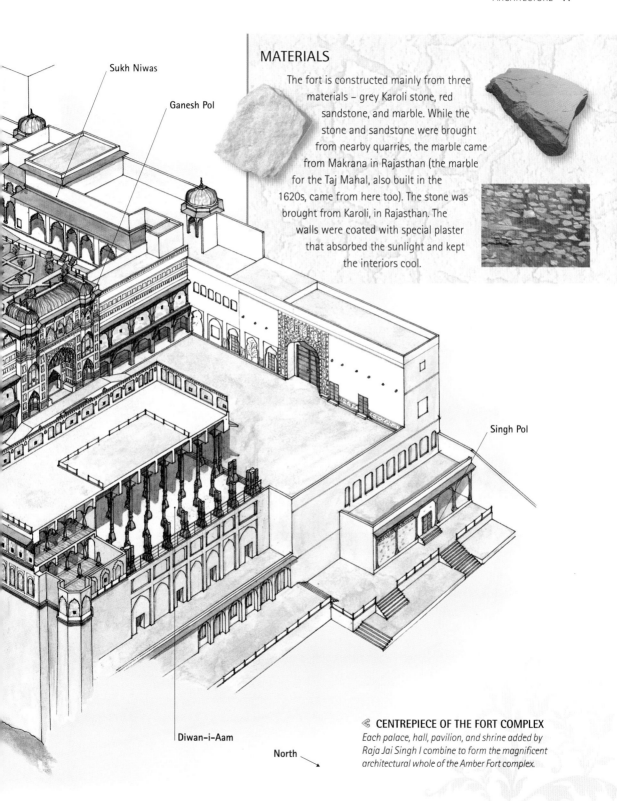

Sukh Niwas

Ganesh Pol

MATERIALS

The fort is constructed mainly from three materials – grey Karoli stone, red sandstone, and marble. While the stone and sandstone were brought from nearby quarries, the marble came from Makrana in Rajasthan (the marble for the Taj Mahal, also built in the 1620s, came from here too). The stone was brought from Karoli, in Rajasthan. The walls were coated with special plaster that absorbed the sunlight and kept the interiors cool.

Singh Pol

Diwan-i-Aam

North

✥ CENTREPIECE OF THE FORT COMPLEX
Each palace, hall, pavilion, and shrine added by Raja Jai Singh I combine to form the magnificent architectural whole of the Amber Fort complex.

Diwan-i-Aam

A pavilion open on three sides, the Diwan-i-Aam (Hall of Public Audience) stands on a raised platform. This is where the rulers received the people and heard their complaints and petitions. It consists of rows of 40 columns that are capped by carved brackets in different shapes. The outer columns are made of red sandstone while the inner ones are made of whitish grey marble. The ceiling rises towards a central rectangle, producing a canopy-like effect.

ORNATE BRACKETS

Red sandstone and white marble brackets top the columns in the Diwan-i-Aam. Elaborately carved, they display a variety of Rajput motifs, such as lotus buds, elephants, or heads of aquatic monsters with curling snouts.

⚜ MAIN HALL
A chandelier and hand-controlled pulleys for fans were suspended from the hooks on the vaulted ceiling.

❦ DIWAN-I-AAM
This imposing hall was built by Raja Jai Singh I.

MOTIFS IN SANDSTONE AND MARBLE

latticed screens

carved brackets

Sattais Kacheri

Next to the Diwan-i-Aam is the administrative court called Sattais Kacheri (*sattais* means 27 and *kacheri* means court), its name derived from the fact that 27 superintendents would spend hours here supervising the governance of the kingdom. This is where the scribes would sit to record revenue petitions and present them to the rulers. The fluted columns and cusped arches are characteristic of Rajput architecture. To the right of the Sattais Kacheri lie the *hammams*, or royal baths, while a row of *jharokhas* overlook the courtyard below. From the other side of this hall is a beautiful view of the Maota Lake and the gardens.

❧ DECORATED COLONNADES
The columns are made of plaster of lime and marble dust burnished to a gloss, to give it a marble-like finish.

JHAROKHA ❧
Small jharokhas *line the second storey of the Sattais Kacheri, with tiny, arched openings to look out from.*

terrace where celebrations were held on full moon nights

❧ OPEN HALL
The arched hall opens out to the courtyard and gardens.

Ganesh Pol wall

Ganesh Pol

In the same courtyard as the Sattais Kacheri, stands the magnificent Ganesh Pol. A three-storeyed gateway, it was constructed in 1640 by Raja Jai Singh I as a ceremonial gate for royal processions. The Ganesh Pol is the most ornate gateway in the Amber Fort. Lavishly painted in the vibrant hues of natural dyes, it is decorated in a remarkable fusion of styles, featuring typical Rajasthani motifs, such as gods and goddesses, and Mughal designs, such as geometric patterns and stylized flowers encircled with foliage. The gateway leads into an open courtyard, where the royal apartments are arranged around a beautiful garden.

⚶ IMAGE OF LORD GANESHA
Above the doorway is a painting of a seated figure of Ganesha – the elephant-headed god after whom the Ganesh Pol is named.

❦ VAULTED CEILING
The arched vaults of the ceiling are painted with elaborate, colourful floral and leaf motifs.

GATEWAY WALLS ❦
Covered with fine frescoes and mosaic work, the walls are pierced by arched windows and doorways.

gilded finial _____

SCREEN DETAIL

floral motif

Suhag Mandir

The uppermost portion of the Ganesh Pol is called the Suhag Mandir (*suhag* means good fortune). It is a small pavilion with projecting balconies screened by delicately carved marble *jaalis* from where women, while remaining unseen, could watch royal processions in the courtyard below. It has octagonal rooms on each side that open out into the balconies.

Suhag Mandir

ARCHED OPENINGS
Windows in the screens are cut out of the jaalis.

painted ceiling

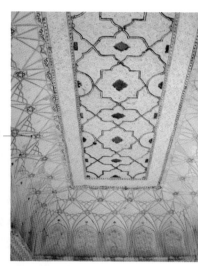

CEILING OF SUHAG MANDIR

THE POL

At a time when every kingdom was considered vulnerable to attacks or invasion, fortification was a prime concern. In the Rajput forts and palaces, the *pol* served just such a purpose. The word *pol* is derived from the Sanskrit word *pratoli,* meaning gateway or entrance to an enclosed area. A *pol* guarded the town, which had only one or two such gateways, the other entrances being secret from outsiders. The *pols* often display intricately carved façades and fresco work on the walls.

⬙ INTERIOR OF SHEESH MAHAL
The arabesque designs and floral motifs on the ceiling are inlaid with mirror slivers.

ROYAL CHAMBERS ⬙
Arched doorways and halls lead to the private apartments of the king.

Sheesh Mahal

Tiny, glittering shards of mirror cover the ceiling and walls of this palace, giving it the name Sheesh Mahal (*sheesh* means mirror and *mahal* means palace). It is also known as Diwan-i-Khas (Hall of Private Audience) as the king met high-ranking nobles and merchants here in the central hall, which is surrounded by a verandah. Since the Sheesh Mahal was built during Raja Jai Singh's time, it is also referred to as Jai Mandir. The inner rooms comprised the winter palace of Raja Jai Singh – thick velvet drapes and mirrors reflecting the light and heat of the oil lamps kept these rooms warm.

MIRROR WORK ⬙
The flowers seem to end in scorpions' tails, a typical Rajasthani motif.

⬙ MARBLE RELIEF
Mughal floral designs are combined with butterflies, another Rajasthani motif.

⚜ SHEESH MAHAL VERANDAH
The stately verandah of the Sheesh Mahal, embellished with marble panels and mirror work, formed part of the personal apartments of the ruler.

Jas Mandir

Above the Sheesh Mahal is the Jas Mandir, the summer palace of Raja Jai Singh. Crowned by a curved roof and *chhatris*, its ceiling is decorated with elegant alabaster relief work and glass inlay. It has fine marble screens overlooking the Maota Lake. Here, cool breezes from the lake would waft in through screens lined with *khus* (fragrant grass), scenting the air.

⚜ CAPITAL
Stylized petal shapes arranged in tiers decorate the capitals of the double columns; the columns support the arches of the Mahal's verandah.

ARABESQUE MOTIF

⚜ CURVED CEILING
Geometric designs give way to floral patterns where the ceiling curves up in the main hall of the Sheesh Mahal.

⌂ **PLEASURE GARDEN**
Water channels laid out in pleasing geometrical patterns adorn the Aram Bagh, which is enclosed by a latticed marble balustrade.

Sukh Niwas and Aram Bagh

The Sukh Niwas (*sukh* means peace and *niwas* means house) is set on the opposite side of the Sheesh Mahal. It consists of a central chamber with marble rooms for the queens on either side. The doors of the rooms are carved from fragrant sandalwood, inlaid with ivory. In front of the Sukh Niwas lies a formal Mughal-style garden called the Aram Bagh (Garden of Leisure). The queens would spend many hours in these gardens, which were decorated with fountains and pools filled with coloured water.

vases painted in varied colours

COOLING DEVICE ⊗
Breeze from latticed conduits would cool the water cascading down marble screens.

⌂ **ENGRAVINGS ON WALLS**
Vases, unlike similar Mughal-style motifs, are engraved without handles.

ARAM BAGH ⊗
This garden, divided into quadrants by geometric paths and waterways, follows the same plan as the Mughal gardens.

Maota Lake and the gardens

Perched on a high hill, the Amber Fort overlooks the Maota Lake, which was the main source of water for the palaces within the fort and also served as a moat to protect the kingdom from intruders. It has three well-planned gardens, with flowerbeds laid out in geometrical patterns. The Kesar Kyari Bagh, with its star-shaped *kyari* (flowerbeds) where *kesar* (saffron) and other exotic plants and herbs were grown, is one of them. These floating gardens (they were hollowed beneath to keep the gardens cool in summer), were the venues for entertainment. Now, the breathtaking and very informative *Son-et-lumiere* (Sound and Light) show takes place here, using the fort as a backdrop.

SAFFRON – THE SPICE OF LIFE

For centuries, fragrant, delicate orange saffron, extracted from the saffron crocus (*Crocus sativus*) flower, has been the spice of life in many parts of India, gracing the feasts of kings and wealthy nobles. The flower has three orange stigmas and a yellow style. These are handpicked, dried, and used to colour and flavour food. It is the most expensive spice in the world.

PULLEY SYSTEM
Water stored in underground tanks was pumped up by pulleys to irrigate the gardens.

FLOWERBEDS
Rare plants were grown in aesthetically laid out, symmetrical rows of hexagonal, stone-bordered flowerbeds.

✿ TWELVE PILLARS
The Baradari is named after its 12 pillars (bara means 12) and the 12 rooms that surround it.

Baradari

A high wall separates the palace of Raja Man Singh I from Jai Singh's palace. The *zenana* (women's quarters) of Man Singh's palace is the oldest part of the palace complex. The Baradari, a colonnaded pavilion, sits in the spectacular courtyard surrounding the *zenana* and it was here that the queens would enjoy performances of music and dance.

THE MUGHAL INFLUENCE

The layout of a typical Rajput palace shows similarities with those of the Mughals based on their shared views of the nature of kingship, courtly life, and the status of women. Elements like domes and arches, and features like quadrilateral gardens, *zenana* apartments, audience chambers such as the Diwan-i-Aam, are Mughal concepts of architecture that have been absorbed by the Rajputs and blended with their own style.

DIWAN-I-AAM, RED FORT

✦ ARCHED COLONNADE
Graceful pillars support the cusped arches of the Baradari; flowing curtains were draped here as screens for the queens.

The Zenana

The *zenana* apartments, where Raja Man Singh's 12 wives and concubines lived, line all four sides of the courtyard. The guards were eunuchs as no man except the king himself could enter this area. Bearing the distinct stamp of Mughal *zenana* architecture, it consists of high walls, long galleries, as well as covered balconies and screened areas from where the royal ladies could watch cultural activities held in the courtyard. The (now faded) murals on the walls depict Krishna Leela (visualization of Lord Krishna's life) scenes.

⊛ ENCLOSURE
Arched doorways entered from a small enclosed courtyard lead into the zenana.

⊰ APARTMENT
A hall in the private chambers of the royal ladies.

⊰ ROYAL CHAMBER
Man Singh's room is situated beside the zenana *apartments.*

RANG MAHAL ⊱
The exquisite Rang Mahal was used by Man Singh I for festivities.

Regal city

Known as the Pink City for the colour many of its buildings were painted in, Jaipur is a fascinating labyrinth of opulent palaces and vibrant bazaars. It was Sawai Raja Jai Singh II who supervised the building of this well-planned city, which took six years after 1727 to complete. Its signature building is the five-storeyed Hawa Mahal (Palace of Winds), with its ornate façade of projecting balconies and perforated screens. Other attractions include the Jantar Mantar (Jai Singh II's astronomical observatory) and the eighteenth-century City Palace (now the City Palace Museum), built in a superb blend of Rajput and Mughal styles. To the south of the City Palace is the bustling Tripolia Bazaar (Triple-arched Market), with the Badi Chaupar (Large Square) at one end. This is where artisans fashion and sell puppets, silver jewellery, pottery, and other handicrafts, and an amazing array of fabrics, flowers, and souvenirs is on offer. For those who prefer tranquillity, the picturesque Jal Mahal (Water Palace) is the place to visit (on the road from Jaipur to Amber). Built in the mid-18th century by Madho Singh I, it has a terrace garden enclosed by arched passages, and at each corner is a semi-octagonal tower capped by an elegant cupola.

⚜ PALACE ON A LAKE
During the monsoon, when water fills the Man Sagar Lake, the Jal Mahal seems to float gently.

JAIGARH FORT

Around the Amber Fort

Guarding the approach from the north to both Amber and Jaipur are a number of forts, the most spectacular of which are Jaigarh and Nahargarh. Perched high on craggy hills and encircled with battlemented walls, they recall a bygone age when warriors fought for supremacy.

Jaigarh

Watching over Amber is Jaigarh (Victory Fort), its great, crenellated walls delineating a sharp ridge for 3km (2 miles). It is connected to Amber through fortified passages. Within the fort is one of the world's few surviving cannon foundries. Its most prized possession is the Jai Van, cast in 1726 and perhaps the world's largest cannon on wheels. Its 6m (20ft) long barrel has carvings of elephants, birds, and flowers.

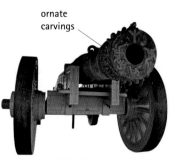

ornate carvings

⚜ JAI VAN
Despite its impressive size, this cannon remained a work of art and was never fired.

Nahargarh

The forbidding Nahargarh (Tiger Fort) was one of the strongholds of the fierce Meena tribe, rulers of this region until they were defeated by the Kachhwahas. Legend says that this was the site of the cenotaph of Nahar Singh, a martyred Rajput warrior, whose spirit resisted all construction until a priest performed tantric rites. In the late 19th century, Madho Singh II added a lavish palace called Madhavendra Bhavan for his nine queens. Laid out in a maze of terraces and courtyards, it has a well-ventilated upper chamber from which the royal ladies could view the city.

Tourist information

Amber is situated on the Delhi-Jaipur highway, 261km from Delhi; 11km from Jaipur, Rajasthan. **By Air:** Options are available for travellers who wish to fly to Jaipur from major cities in India. Contact the respective airlines or tour operators. **By Rail:** Trains to Jaipur run from all the major cities in India. The Shatabdi Express has daily services between Delhi and Jaipur. For enquiries, visit www.indianrail.gov.in. **By Road:** Jaipur is connected by road to many major cities of India. **To Amber:** Buses, luxury coaches, and taxis are available on hire between Jaipur and Amber.

Visitor's checklist

The best time to visit Amber is between October and February. The Amber Fort is open to visitors from 9am to 5pm every day. The entrance fee for citizens of India is Rs 25 per head, and Rs 150 for foreigners (camera charges are included). Audio Guides in various languages are available for a fee at the Entry Ticket Counter or the Audio Guide Room located at Diwan-i-Aam. For updates on fees and timings, visit www.rajasthantourism.gov.in. Here are a few things you need to carry when travelling in India.

⤳ Drinking water, torch, map or guidebook, mosquito repellent, loose change, sunblock

⤳ First aid kit, medication for tropical diseases like diarrhoea, dysentery, and malaria, water purification tablets

⤳ Light cotton clothes in summer, woollens in winter; hat, umbrella or raincoat, easy-to-remove footwear

⤳ Credit cards or travellers' cheques (optional, but advisable)

JAIPUR & EASTERN RAJASTHAN

Publisher's acknowledgements

Dorling Kindersley and Penguin Books India would like to thank the following people for their help and guidance in preparing this book:
Dr Narayani Gupta and Ranjana Sengupta for reviewing the text so painstakingly; Punita Singh, Manager, Rough Guides India, for getting us permission to use the maps in the book; Jayaprakash Mishra of Rough Guides India and Suresh Kumar of DK Travel Guides for helping us with the maps.

Picture credits

The publishers are grateful to the following individuals, picture libraries, and companies for permission to reproduce their photographs.

Bryn Walls 19b, 22cl/t. **DK Images** 7br/cr, 9br, 11tl, 12br, 19cra, 22bl. **DK Travel Guides** 5c, 10/11c. **Gary Ombler** 1c, 3c, 4/5t, 6/7t, 8ca, 9tl/c, 12cl, 12/13bl, 13tl/cr/br, 14/15bl, 15ftl/tl, 16tl, 16br, 17bl/tr.bc, 18t/clb, 20/21tl. **India Picture Agency** 7cr. **Rohan Sinha** 6/7bc, 8/9bc, 11cra/tr, 12cra, 15cr, 16bl, 16/17t, 18br/cr, 19cla, 20bl, 21bl/br/c/tr. **Rough Guides** 24cr. **Sanjay Austa** 20crb.

Abbreviations key: a=above, b=bottom, c=centre, f=far, l=left, t=top, r=right

Jacket Image: **Gary Ombler**.

Notes